FRESH STARTS

TRANSFORMATION IN ACTION

CAMILLE LEON

BALBOA.PRESS
A DIVISION OF HAY HOUSE

Balboa Press books may be ordered through booksellers or by contacting:

Balboa Press
A Division of Hay House
1663 Liberty Drive
Bloomington, IN 47403
www.balboapress.com
844-682-1282

Because of the dynamic nature of the Internet, any web addresses or links contained in this book may have changed since publication and may no longer be valid. The views expressed in this work are solely those of the author and do not necessarily reflect the views of the publisher, and the publisher hereby disclaims any responsibility for them.

The author of this book does not dispense medical advice or prescribe the use of any technique as a form of treatment for physical, emotional, or medical problems without the advice of a physician, either directly or indirectly. The intent of the author is only to offer information of a general nature to help you in your quest for emotional and spiritual well-being. In the event you use any of the information in this book for yourself, which is your constitutional right, the author and the publisher assume no responsibility for your actions.

Any people depicted in stock imagery provided by Getty Images are models, and such images are being used for illustrative purposes only.
Certain stock imagery © Getty Images.

Cover tattoo courtesy of Adam Kilss.

Holistic Chamber of Commerce logo by Michelle Del Rey.

Roots image courtesy of Yves Bodson.

Print information available on the last page.

ISBN: 978-1-9822-5929-7 (sc)
ISBN: 978-1-9822-5931-0 (hc)
ISBN: 978-1-9822-5930-3 (e)

Library of Congress Control Number: 2020923129

Balboa Press rev. date: 01/05/2021

Dedicated to

you!

Cheryl ♡ ン

Thank you so much
for being part of our
HCC fresh start!

Camille
2021

AUTHOR NOTES AND APPRECIATION

Special thanks to my parents, Linda and Marik, for their openness to growth and the shifts of our relationships over the years.

Carol Ann, our friendship is special, and our laughter is rich. Thank you!

Peggy and Blanche, you are unexpected blessings. I love you!

David, Kelsey, Sierra—I'm so glad you are part of my whole fam damily!

Adam Telanoff, Barbara Schiffman, Chantalynn Huynh, Charn Pennewaert, Dawna Jakubecy, Denise Lewis Premschak, Dianne Russell, Don Miller, Dr. Sherrie Reimers, Gerrit Kruidhof, Heather Potvin, Karen Sachs, Lainie Sevante Wulkan, Lauren Kelly, Lesly Nunez, Neal Bychek, Paul Cholak, Rene Segal Stern, Sara Munshin, Sharla Jacobs, Shayla Mihaly, Theresa Callard-Moore and especially Tiana Minor, I am so thankful for your presence in my life and your part in bringing this vision of help and healing to reality. I could not have done this without you.

Thank you to the many healers of mind, body, spirit, business, budget, and planet who are here to help us all, especially those of you who are early members of the Holistic Chamber of Commerce (HCC). You bring dreams to life.

Holistic Chamber of Commerce logo icon

Once the deeper layers of my inner self were revealed and healed, I found joy in unexpected spaces and places. For my new joy-based community, thank you for helping me remember how to dance!

CONTENTS

THE JOURNEY TO JOY

I was a mess—heartbroken and in pain, emotionally and otherwise, though you wouldn't have known it to look at me.

Some sadness requires more than a pill to cure.

Real change takes time and lasts a lifetime. It also requires help and healing from many sources.

Evolution is uncomfortable.

Real change is messy.

Whether it is your body or your business, when you are actively engaged in transforming your life, there likely will be times when you question what's next. These moments are when your roots grow stronger.

At a deep level, I knew to seek holistic and natural healers to help guide my journey to a healthier and happier life. This book is the true story of that transformation from darkness to light.

A note about holism: From my point of view, holism is not just about health and healing or even mind/body/spirit. Holistic professionals, practitioners, and businesses balance long-term consequences with short-term results. What I do or say today lays the foundation for tomorrow. What you choose to do or say today lays the foundation for your tomorrow, and it has a ripple effect into my life as well. This applies to attorneys and accountants as much as it does to healers and yoga instructors. Those in more traditional professions—be they webmasters or real estate agents—can do important work in keeping someone stress-free. Likewise, energy healers can help us stay in touch with (and heal) our deeper influences and feelings, especially the hurts from the not-so-forgotten past.

Holism includes eco-friendly options because the healthier you are as a person, the healthier you want your environment to be—inside your home and outside in the community where you live, from the air you breathe to the artwork on your walls.

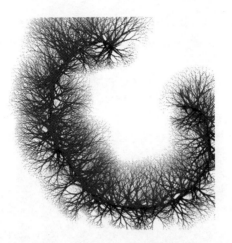

Exploring our roots and connections

The available blank space in this book invites *you* to

write,
draw,
play,
dream,
and design the next stage of *your* life,

jot down new ideas and connections to manifest
in your mind and life,
and let them take root and grow.

I—and the universe—invite you to transform yourself.

Mind * Body * Spirit *
Business * Budget * Planet

Time and money,
health and wealth,
relationships and resources
are all connected
with love.

After too many false starts, I am ready for a fresh start! Are you?

Indulge yourself for a short minute in the sadness of your past: domestic abuse, child abuse, rape, victimhood, bullying, obesity, diabetes, disease, bad choices, bad boyfriends (or girlfriends), belligerent bosses, poverty/scarcity, famine, anger, resentment, frustration, disease, war—whatever it was for you.

Write it all down. Get it on paper and out of your system.

Use a timer and set it for five to fifteen minutes—max.

Now stop!

Move on.

Indulge yourself in the fresh starts you create today: peace, joy, love, abundance, dancing, music, art, creativity, fun, friends, family, health, income, good relationships, smart decisions, and both long- and short-term success. Recognize that lessons learned are in the past and can stay there. Find joy and gratitude in your present circumstances.

What would you like your future to be?

Come with me on this wonderful and wild journey of transformation!

This book is filled with short essays, stories, questions, and meditations to help you keep moving forward in each and every way on each and every day.

STEP 1

THE JOURNEY

DYSFUNCTION JUNCTION

Let's get real for a minute. I'm the woman who didn't just want to find healing for herself. Feeling broken, I wanted to cover the entire planet with healers, connecting them to provide help for everyone all over. I sat alone most days, except when I was on the job in a workplace designed to keep people at arm's length while feigning connection. I was surrounded by ex-felons (those who'd committed misdemeanors need not apply), addicts, alcoholics, homeless people, domestic violence survivors, and a mash-up of others more broken than I was.

Some people seem broken because they care so much and feel so deeply. They hide their feelings behind alcohol, drugs, bravado, rules, judgments, and submission. Mostly, these are ways to hide and protect themselves from further damage and despair.

For me, this included an angry mother and a scared father, both lost. (It's not my place to tell their stories. Perhaps they were too young when I was born, still learning to be adults and in no position to care for me.) Two ex-husbands and a lot of one-night stands. No children. That second divorce left me feeling damaged, mired in debt, and doubting my ability to dig out.

My journey was … messy. I woke up one day and realized I was thirty-nine-ish. Living a bit like a college student, renting in someone else's house. I had a good job but wasn't happy.

Ugh.

I woke up a few years later and was older, a bit better off. My work life was better, while my personal life was still a mess or nonexistent, depending on the day.

I've been raped. My mother beat me. My dad left when I was young—too young—and unable to comprehend anything beyond the emotions of it. The emotions of a toddler are raw and unfiltered. They sit like a seed in the belly and the heart and the brain.

I was angry, frustrated, sad, in pain, resentful—a mixed bag of ugliness under a cool surface of control.

When I finally woke up, I realized I wasn't alone.

Other people—perhaps you—have had painful childhoods or broken relationships, have suffered from unexpected situations that caused stress or even posttraumatic stress disorder (PTSD).

There are healers in this world who move us from judgment of ourselves and others, through forgiveness, to love, even to fun and joy because once we are healed from our pasts, where do we go from there? Fill your life with light so there is less room for darkness. Shadows will come and go, and you will always find your way back to the light.

A lot more people need access to that healing, the healing that goes deep enough to pull out old roots and plant new seeds.

Remember that you are you. You are not your parents, siblings, or children. You may share traits in common with family members but that doesn't mean that everything is the same. Explore and discover what works best for you.

For me, I first had to learn to say no to all the things (and people) that weren't good for me. It took many years and a ton of practice. The more you practice *no*, the easier it gets.

It was like acknowledging that driving through the back alley was bad for my car. It was full of potholes, and it stressed the shocks and punctured my tires. After I decided to start avoiding the alley and take the paved and well-maintained streets instead, I still turned into the alley at least once a day for the next five days. It was a habit, learned from repetition. It had become my routine to turn there, and it took five days before I consistently avoided the potholes altogether by taking the *second* turn instead of the first.

The same was true for my life. It took time, once I was even aware of how my choices had placed me where I was, to make new choices and receive the rich results and rewards that flowed from them.

Unfortunately, most lifestyle habits have been habits for too long and will take more than five days to change.

THE DOWNWARD SPIRAL

One trigger
Can remind me
That
I'm not
Where I want to be,
And into the
Rabbit hole I go.

What's the key to significant long-term change and transformation? Stay supported! Surround yourself with people on a similar journey. After a few months of working as a coach, I felt alone and overwhelmed. *How do I juggle my time and prioritize my commitments? How do I manage my money?* Starting the Holistic Chamber of Commerce connected me with fellow professionals who faced similar challenges. For some, joining a Sunday morning fellowship group is a better idea.

Find the group that is best for you so you can share your experiences, insights, and ideas with others, and listen as they share too.

STEP 2

THE DANCE

Left step,
Right step,
Rock step.

Let me go on record as saying that living life—and especially starting and running a business—is quite a bit like swing dancing. To be specific, East Coast swing, which has a left-step, right-step, rock-step pattern. The rock step is when you step backward to "rock" and then forward to reconnect with your partner.

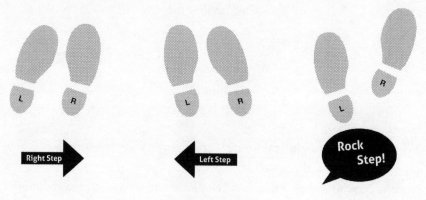

Doing the footwork

To be a good swing dancer, you must always be in partnership with someone else. To be a good entrepreneur and business owner, you must always be in partnership. Whom you are partnered with may be different from day to day: customers, clients, vendors, staff, business partners (if you have any), consultants, economic influences, sales, or expenses. Got it?

Sometimes you lead; other times, be prepared and willing to follow.

It may be messy and awkward. When your partner leads you into a spin, are you ready to pivot?

The more you are present and aware of these elements, the better the dance will go. You will be ready to move and create, rather than halt and break down.

A WIN OR A LESSON

It is always a win or a lesson, which is really a win. In the words of Nelson Mandela, "I never lose. I either win or learn."

Done is better than perfect.

Trust your decision for today. Go ahead and do it! If tomorrow brings new information and you want to make a change or an update, it's all right.

Trust yourself. Have faith in the process, and you'll be fine. Just make sure your process includes action when that is what is called for.

Let go of the doubt, and you'll have more time for everything else that will keep you moving forward.

Is there a project on which you are stalled? Is it almost ready but not quite perfect? Once it is "live," it will be easier to see whether improvements are really needed or if it is A-okay as is.

Write about it here:

WALKING IN CIRCLES

When you want to walk forward, you step first on one foot and then the other, always switching from the left foot to the right foot, alternating all the way.

If you always step forward with the same foot, you will find yourself going in circles.

If you feel like you are going in circles, consider ways you can step forward on the other foot. In other words, switch things up!

STEP 3

GETTING ON THE BRIDGE

In health *and* business, there is always a bridge from where we are to where we are going, whether that is where we are headed, given our current trajectory, or where we want to go when focused on our goals.

Where is your bridge taking you?

If you have weight issues, the bridge is from what you weigh today to what you want to weigh.

If it's health issues, the bridge is from sickness to fitness.

If you're overworked, the bridge is from doing everything on your own to hiring consultants and staff.

If you want to grow your business, the bridge is from one customer/client/patient to ten to one hundred to one thousand or more.

If you are strained, the bridge is from stress to everything you want.

If you feel alone, the bridge is from loneliness to connection, companionship, and love.

If you feel at war, the bridge is to peace.

If you are unhappy, the bridge is to joy.

What bridge(s) do you need? Where do you need to go?

What bridge(s) do you want? Where do you want to go?

In today's world, there are so many options. How do you determine which one is best for you?

CREATING YOUR COURAGE

Significant change requires courage.

Change means getting out of your comfort zone, ongoingly, perhaps even every day.

Friendships and relationships will change; some will get better, and others will go away, as you stop smoking or drinking, treat yourself with respect, stop kowtowing to others, stand up for yourself without belittling others, eat in healthier restaurants, or spend more time doing art, meditating, dancing, exercising, reading.

As you stand up for yourself more often, bullies will go away. Whether it's a boss, friend, or significant other, that person is likely to find someone who is more willing to put up with poor treatment. Let them. Spend your time nurturing new friends, colleagues, coworkers, lovers, and partners. If you are the bully, those who are comfortable in the victim position will leave you too.

Once you let go of the drama of pain and suffering, you'll have time for people and activities that you love. What might those be? Way back when, I was "all work, all the time," and now I have time to dance, have coffee and tea with friends, paint, read, and write this book.

There is no need for delay. More time doing what you love and enjoy, even exploring what that might be, is less time dealing with negativity.

Is it time for you to start exploring? What are you curious to try?

THE EXHILARATION EFFECT

When we are stuck in our lives, it is often because of an underlying fear.

Years ago, when I was forced into several significant changes all at once, I felt like I was being pushed out of an airplane.

I was getting divorced for the second time, moving to a new city, and changing my work (and income source) at the same time.

So that's what I did—I jumped out of an airplane! It was scary and exhilarating.

The world looks different from up there. Very different. There are more possibilities. You see things that you don't see on the ground. And I landed on my feet, knowing that when I keep my eyes open, I can see possibilities that may not be apparent otherwise.

Try it.* You may be amazed at what you can do!

* This is *not* a recommendation to go skydiving. If you have heart or health problems or a fear of heights, do *not* try this. For your first time, especially, tandem jumps are suggested over solo jumps—mine was a tandem jump. Do not attempt this on your own.

Since that jump, ever so long ago, I've kept up the routine of doing scary new things to keep moving forward and understanding the world in new ways. I take the experience of overcoming one fear and apply it to other areas of my life where I want to create courage to take my next step.

Thanks to my good friend and colleague Barbara Schiffman, a certified hypnotherapist, the Exhilaration Effect concepts have been developed further so that others can benefit from these ideas as well. Here are a few of our lessons learned over the years:

If you decide to explore and experiment with the Exhilaration Effect, be sure to work with professionals, when appropriate. All three times that I've jumped out of airplanes, I've gone with a tandem skydive.

Some of the ideas below might work for you too, although they are solely up to you.

➤ Eat exotic foods: When I wanted to shift my perspective from what was "normal," I chose crickets, scorpions, and ants at an Asian-fusion restaurant in Santa Monica. It taught me that some people eat these foods every day. Some people eat them on special occasions as a way to celebrate. Still others don't eat them at all. Are your perspectives on whether something is good or bad based on your childhood? Is it possible that by being open-minded, you can find other approaches that work just as well or better?

➤ Breathe underwater (aka scuba dive): Another game-changer is realizing that we can use technology to do the "impossible." What technology could help you now?

➤ Speed and my NASCAR moment: To learn that I can be safe, even when going faster than ever before, I rented Mesa Marin Raceway in Bakersfield, California, for a day of racing with friends. I spun out during my exit from the pit, and the car stopped when I hit the tire barrier. Fortunately, the five-point seatbelt held tight. No injuries! What are you waiting for?

➤ Speed and my Lamborghini joyride: Do you ever wish that someone else would do the driving? I sure do. It can be tiresome to make all the decisions and feel as if everyone is depending on me to be right. Still, it's fun to go fast, faster, fastest! One day, I found a racetrack in Las Vegas and signed up for a ride-along with a professional driver. Now, I feel ready to let someone else do the driving in other aspects of my life.

If you are a just starting on your transformation adventure, consider milder yet equally significant ways to begin:

Dress differently than you usually do (all black, all color, no makeup, strong makeup).
Meditate (if you never have).
Drive a new way to your office (turn right instead of left).

Remember that done is better than perfect. Perfectionism is just another form of procrastination.

I say this quite a bit. Too many people get stopped while trying to be perfect in whatever they are doing. If it's not your taxes, get it good enough, and let it go. Only then can it really become what it's meant to be. Bill Gates became a multi-gazillionaire with this approach, releasing software and then releasing an update based on fixes that others told him about. By releasing it, it got better and bigger.

When you want new results and rewards, do something new. That is the corollary to "If you do what you've always done, you'll get what you've always gotten."

Is there anything fun and exciting that you would like to do? What is it? Would doing it help you release your hesitation and overcome fear in other areas of your life?

Write about it here:

LEAPS OF FAITH

I'm not sure when it happened that I became a specialist in taking leaps of faith—and for purposes of this book, I'm not sure that it matters.

This is about *your* leap of faith; that jump from where you are to where you want to be, even though you can't see all of the steps in between. There will be times when you feel as if you are climbing a mountain. It looks scary to go forward but you don't want to go back either.

Is it a conversation that you are avoiding? Is it an action that you are resisting?

What is your next leap of faith?

Write about it here:

STAGE 2

TIPS AND TIDBITS

LITTLE LESSONS

This book shares little lessons, not in any particular order.

It would be lovely if life happened in a set and predictable order, if your lessons showed up in the same sequence as mine. Nonetheless, we each have our own paths to walk. While there are similarities between them, the progression is rarely the same.

Life happens all at once, *and* one step at a time. We get in a fight at home, and it may come to the office to influence our work that day. We get stressed at the office, and it comes home with us to weaken our immunity. If we get sick, it affects all our relationships, personal and professional. That, in turn, affects our success (however you define it) in all elements of our lives.

And so these little lessons flow in and out.

Inhale.

Exhale.

Give.

Receive.

Flow creates strength.

Love without money is a tough life.
Money without love is ugly and meaningless.

Balance includes both—
Love and money.

FOUNDATION

It's clear that our economic and political systems need healing as well.

Parts of Wall Street and Washington are broken.

As much as some of us like to talk about inner healing and beauty and wellness as emotional and physical fitness, financial fitness is just as relevant.

Money matters. We have bills to pay, individually and on a larger scale.

How do we connect our money to our values? How do we get healthy in *every* aspect and element of our lives?

In these pages, we will cover some very practical and personal tips about connecting the two.

Note on terminology: you may call someone who purchases your product(s) and/or service(s) a customer, client, or patient. For our purposes here, I often refer to all three.

I think best in little lessons—you know, the kind that are short and to the point. Really, think of it as straightforward and semi-sweet. If that works for you, then you'll love this book.

Warning: My thoughts are not always organized. I often head off on tangents in the middle of conversations. Likewise, some of these may seem out of order to you. Live with it!

Look for the *aha* in here to create the push/pull that propels you forward.

It feels odd for me to write this. I still see that I have so much further to go. Apparently, that is the nature of life and business, especially for those who choose to do something outside of the norm. We can always learn. If you are selling shoes or purses or if you are selling a more traditional service (e.g., legal or financial advice), perhaps the path is easier. I don't know.

Most of my work is with those individuals who have chosen to provide a somewhat uncommon product and/or service, one that is beyond the status quo, outside of conventional mainstream norms.

These days, we see overnight-success stories on a regular basis, so much so that it's tempting to take for granted that the law of attraction works like that. We forget that the law of *attraction* usually works hand in hand with the law of *action* over time. An "overnight success" comes after years of consistent commitment and achievements that build one on another. It's time for us to remember that momentum builds with time and consistent action in pursuit of our goals.

PEOPLE WHO CARE CAN STILL BE UNAWARE

It's that simple. Most people are unaware that they've hurt your feelings. Just as you are often unaware of how you've hurt their feelings.

Give people the benefit of the doubt. Perhaps they didn't do it on purpose to hurt you. From their point of view, it made sense.

It is personal, and it isn't. Sometimes, it *is* all about you. Many times, it is all about the other person. When you get an unexpected response, consider that it has more to do with the other person (even if he or she is blaming you).

Has someone hurt your feelings? Are you resentful or irritated about a relationship? What can you let go of so that the other person (or people) can learn on their own?

Write about it here:

MONEY, HONEY

Whether you want to call it abundance, prosperity, profit, or anything else, on earth, in its raw form, money has a certain *je ne sais quoi* that is specific to itself. Money can buy almost anything. I know people who will set aside their values for money. Of course, in most cases, it takes money to buy (or rent) a place to live, food to eat, clothes to wear, and so on. If you aren't spending your money for these things, you are spending either your time or energy in trade with someone who has the money for them.

Don't get me wrong; it may be a fair exchange. Be honest with yourself. If your parents or your ex is paying for your lifestyle, you are trading some freedom of choice in exchange. If you have earned the money on your own or inherited it, with no strings attached, then money provides the ability to purchase what you want, when you want it. This freedom of choice is unlikely to be had in other ways and can open doors quickly and easily for you.

Interestingly, lack of money also has a type of freedom of choice, in that there are few rules by which the homeless are hampered (unless they want to live in a shelter, most of which are governed by reasonable middle-class rules designed for group-living situations).

I started a chamber of commerce. Commerce is all about the exchange of money for goods or services. If I want something you have (a product or service), I can give you money in exchange for it. When you accept my money, I receive the purchased product/service, as long as you keep your end of the bargain.

When you accept my money, you can then spend it however you want (investing in more of said product, or education, or paying staff/consultants, or paying your rent/mortgage, or buying a yacht, or any number of other options). In other words, doing and having what you want.

If you give your product/service away for free, you eventually will run out of money, unless you have another source of income. If you have inherited money or are supported by income from other sources (real estate, stocks, bonds, alimony, prior investments, lottery winnings, etc.), then you may be able to give your product/service away for free for a long time. Still, any way you look at it, money is part of this equation.

In Matthew 26:11, we read that even Jesus knew that "the poor you will have with you always." He did not say, "You must be poor with them." Or even, "It is more blessed to be poor than rich." These verses are *not* in the Bible, even as the Bible emphasizes the importance of having our priorities in proper order, of putting God before money.

You can have *both*—God and money—in your life.

I grew up in a ghetto in Buffalo, New York. In my world, that was better than living in the projects. The levels of noise, chaos, and pollution in poor neighborhoods (whether ghetto or projects) tend to be higher than those in wealthy neighborhoods.

When the default that you were raised with is poor, it becomes a comfort zone, in that *you know the rules*. You know how to talk to your neighbors, the words to use, the slang to use, and the clothes to wear, depending on how you want people to respond.

That is the shift that is most tricky. When your default is poor, how do you learn new ways of being? How do you learn to accept and receive financial wealth, especially if no one you know has it (except the drug dealers)?

Are you still stuck in the poverty from your past? In what ways can you receive and appreciate abundance in your life today?

Write about it here:

NEW, NEW, NEW

When I moved in 2019 to a new home in a new city in a new state, I started meeting new people and creating new everything: furniture, tchotchkes, friends, habits (exercise! an improv class!), adventures.

It's like more than a breath of fresh air; a wild wind is blowing through my life, just as it is through this planet.

Old ways are getting exposed and disrupted.

New ideas and insights are showing up all over.

It is easy to see the transitional time we are in—shootings, the opioid crisis, wacky weather patterns, scandals among the so-called elite, a crisis called COVID-19, and more.

At the same time, we have more opportunities than ever before. The internet has opened doors to possibilities previously overpriced, unseen, and unexplored.

It is now possible to make money by pursuing your passion and your purpose, whether that is art, fancy coffee, health foods, yoga, Legos, essential oils—you name it!

How do I know this? I see it more and more every day, and I am doing it myself. It has been a journey, a winding and wonderful road from there to here, and it keeps getting better every day.

How can you flip this switch for yourself?

When did I flip mine?

Was it after my second divorce? That first jump from an airplane? After 9/11? Leaving my corporate job? That first meeting of my beta-test local-only Holistic Chamber of Commerce? The trip to China with my mother?

Each day brings a new opportunity to choose anew and flip that switch. All these experiences—and others—have flipped switches for me and helped create a more beautiful and bountiful life.

You can do the same.

We all have many moments and opportunities to make different and new choices, to choose another way, to disrupt our current trajectories and head off in a healthier and happier direction. You can create a bridge for yourself and invite your family and friends to come along, step by step.

Don't get me wrong. Some people will not leave their comfort zones or let go of habits born from years of familiarity. They say the same words at the same times to the same people, perpetuating what they already know. Too often, we believe that the devil we know is better than the one we don't. It seems safer to be guided by the fear that anything else might be worse than what we have now.

What if it gets better? This is not to say that there won't be difficult days ahead. Most likely, there will be. When you are climbing a mountain, there are times when it looks scary to go forward and ugly to go back. Choosing between a rock and a hard place is no fun.

Still, the view from the top? A place where miracles happen every day? It's worth it!

What switches are you ready to flip?

Write about it here:

ROUTINES

Is it a rotten rut or a healthy habit?

Are you stuck in a rut, or are your routines helping you? If you say *I always* or *I never*, then it is probably a rut. If you are open to trying new ways, then it's a good approach.

God, grant me the serenity to let go of my rotten ruts,
The courage to hold on to my healthy habits,
And the wisdom to know the difference.

Routines can be helpful!

But some routines are really ruts in disguise that keep you stuck in an old comfort zone. Even if it was useful in the past, it may not be helping you now.

Look at the actions you take and the words you use automatically—you know, your default auto-response.

If it's time to let go of it, stop. Hold still. Come up with a new response, a new routine, even if it is as simple as taking more time to consider the best response.

THE SLINGSHOT EFFECT

This is when you pull back in order to propel yourself forward at a super-fast speed. Usually, it results from circumstances that seem to push you back.

Consider that it may be a gift, a chance to review and consider what's best now, at this stage, for your forward movement.

Like a bow and arrow or a slingshot, let it create momentum so you can shoot toward the heavens to hit your target.

Is there an area of your life where you feel like you are being pushed backward or forced to cut back? Can you see a silver lining that could come from trimming the fat in that area?

Write about it here:

THE LOVE LIST

In writing my chapter for *Inspired Wisdom Word Search*, it was clear that I was busy. As I got busier with a variety of tasks, I got more irritated, as it all seemed overwhelming.

It was clearly time to look at my to-do list and make some major revisions.

We *all* have twenty-four hours in a day. How do we prioritize and choose how to use our time? How do *you* choose what gets your attention?

If you are like most people I know, you have a certain set of given responsibilities every day. Perhaps you are married or living with someone or raising children. Maybe you have a job or are running a business.

Do you keep a to-do list to manage the different details involved in living life and prioritizing your days?

What if you treated this as your "love list" and let it remind you why you do what you do? Could this reframe the things you do so that you recognize how it supports you and your loved ones and how much you already love your life?

Let go of your to-do list that is filled with problems to solve and allow your "love list" to evolve into the solutions you are creating. Find others who can help you with the tasks that are less fun for you. Then, you can focus on what you love and do what you do best!

What is the first thing you usually do on any given day? Is it the most important thing? Is it the most fun? What would happen if you reprioritized your days, according to importance or joy?

Write about it here:

ONENESS AND DUALITY

When I was a young woman, I experienced a great deal of internal conflict, doubting myself often and feeling torn between two extremes. Looking at my parents, I felt like I was at odds with myself, caught in a struggle between fire and water.

One day, a close friend asked if I could come up with times when fire and water worked together to create a powerful result. At the time, I couldn't come up with anything.

Here's what he gave me next:

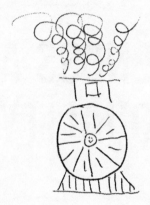

Fire and water are powerful together.

His drawing showing the power of fire and water when they are working together opened my eyes to a divergent view on these two elements and to an unfamiliar view of myself. I could be powerful by discovering ways for my internal opposites to blend with each other.

Oneness and duality bring balance in many areas of our lives. Life, health, and business are all about the interplay of opposites.

Is there a situation where you feel torn between two opposing options? Is it a relationship or a situation? Is there another person involved or just up to you? Is there one thing you can do today that will free things up for another step forward tomorrow?

Write about it here:

WHEN DO YOU TAKE ACTION?
WHEN DO YOU WAIT WITH FAITH?

> ➤ I sent an email once, trying to get new people to sign up for membership, and then started calling them right away to make sure they got it. The problem with that? My recipients needed time to read through the email and sign up. I needed to wait and give them a chance to take action on their end.

Is there a situation in your life right now where you have recently taken action and now need to wait for results? What about a situation where you have waited too long (procrastination) and now need to take action?

Write about it here:

WHEN DO YOU SAY SOMETHING? WHEN DO YOU STAY SILENT AND LISTEN?

➢ There are times, especially when negotiating an agreement, when it is helpful to add your comments. It is also smart to wait in silence, listening as the other person clarifies his or her perspective and goals. When everyone has spoken, it is easier to create a win/win solution.

Is there a relationship in your life right now in which you have been too quiet, not saying what needs to be said? Is there one in which you have been too vocal, oversharing your opinions and complaints, without waiting for (or accepting) the other person's response?

Write about it here:

WHEN DO YOU GO ONLINE? WHEN DO YOU GO IN PERSON?

➢ Are you an introvert or an extrovert? It is tempting to stick with our default modes. When I have a general message that I want to send to everyone all at once, I can do it faster and more effectively by going online. If it's important to get a specific response from a particular person, I know that picking up the phone is an excellent way to make it more personal. At other times, having a cup of tea together is the best bet.

➢ This question is also relevant for sticky situations: When I want someone to digest my concerns and have time to respond thoughtfully, I will often send an email. But some of my friends prefer to talk things through together. When we are face-to-face, there is an emotional element that will *sometimes* open the door for a better outcome.

Is there a message you want to share with others right now? How many people do you want to share it with? Is there anyone from whom you want a specific response? What is the best way to share your message with them?

Write about it here:

WHEN DO YOU FOCUS ON INCREASING INCOME? WHEN DO YOU REVIEW YOUR EXPENSES TO CUT COSTS?

➤ Only you can answer this. Your focus often determines the results you receive. The questions you ask lead to the answers you receive. "Is there a way to sell more of these?" brings different answers than "How do I pay this month's rent?"

During the early years for the Holistic Chamber of Commerce, it was important to check our bank balance often to see which bills could be paid. Once we were further along, it became more meaningful to meditate and contemplate new possibilities for partnerships and raising revenue.

What are your most pressing financial concerns today? What does your personal and/or business budget look like? When are your next bills due, and is there enough money to cover them? Where should your financial focus be?

Write about it here:

WHERE IS THE BALANCE BETWEEN FAITH AND ACTION? HOW DO YOU FIND IT FOR YOURSELF?

➤ Life is lived on a time line. It is a process of learning, and we all have our own lessons. Reading books like this one and connecting with your support network can help you find the balance that is best for you.

➤ Only you know if you are hesitating out of fear or waiting in faith. These may look the same to an outside observer. Only you know your truth.

Is there any area of your life where you feel stuck? What actions can you take today in order to shift your tomorrow? How does faith play a role in this area?

Write about it here:

WHEN DO YOU CUT BACK IN ORDER TO EXPAND?

➤ To grow a garden, you have to prune the plants and do periodic weeding. To find what you are looking for, it's helpful to declutter your home and/or office every so often. Cutting unnecessary expenses leaves more money available for what you really want, just as watching less television gives you more time for exercise or play or family.

What is something that you could cut back on that would give you more of what you really want?

Write about it here:

WITH SOLITUDE AND COMMUNITY

➢ As much as community can help you discover and explore your options and opportunities, it is your life. When you have enough input, meditate and contemplate to decide for yourself. After all, you are the one who has to live with the consequences.

There is a scene in the 2009 film *Invictus* in which the Nelson Mandela character, played by Morgan Freeman, decides to go ahead with a course of action, despite the advice of his inner circle. It is a powerful reminder of what it takes to commit to yourself and the course of action that makes the most sense for *you*.

Success calls for a mix of approaches. What worked yesterday may not work today. What works with one person may not work with another—which you know because what works to get what you want from your mother is different from what works with your father.

There are times when you are the only one who can consider the various factors involved and come up with a strong solution.

At other times, the input, ideas, and insights of others can add immense value to your process. To ignore the information and inspiration that others share is to miss out on perspectives that could shift your mindset and your success, quickly and easily.

What decision is on your plate now? Do you have enough input to decide and move forward?

Write about it here:

WITH MOVEMENT AND STILLNESS

➤ When you are in business, most days, some action is required, whether it is a social media post, or a phone call, or a report to review. Still, most successful entrepreneurs and business owners have some of their biggest and brightest ideas when they are meditating or relaxing by taking a walk. Even napping can provide much-needed rejuvenation to create powerful productivity when you get back to the project on your plate.

To do one without the other is limiting.

How do you know when to do which? Being aware of and honest about today's circumstances will help you decide what makes the most sense, given a specific situation. Awareness is not the same as being honest about what is really going on. Most of us know people who are aware that they have poor eating habits and shouldn't be eating fast food, yet they are not honest with themselves about the impact that has on their health.

Do you have a comfort zone between these two extremes on the spectrum? Perhaps you are always moving and looking for something to do, or you sit still too often, waiting for someone else to take the lead. How can you create a better balance for yourself?

Write about it here:

CONVERSATIONS AND QUESTIONS

WHAT MONEY DOESN'T BUY:
Health

WHAT MONEY DOES BUY:
Fresh, Organic Food
Acupuncture
Chiropractic

WHAT MONEY DOESN'T BUY:
Love

WHAT MONEY DOES BUY:
Amusement park with the kids
Coffee with a friend
BBQ for the family

WHAT MONEY DOESN'T BUY:
Compassion

WHAT MONEY DOES BUY:
Donation to a favorite cause
Meal for someone in need
Time to help someone

HOW ARE YOU STAYING IN BALANCE?

What money does and doesn't buy

What are the complementary and integrative health and wellness techniques that can help you?

Human nature is such that we often look for a quick fix to know what will take care of our perceived problem(s) right away.

Sometimes known as *holistic*, the techniques and specialties here work on their own, as well as hand in hand with Western allopathic methods for healing illness and recovering from injuries. They are also used on their own, as a means of preventing illness in the first place.

Many of the following suggestions are also tools for personal development and transformation. If any resonate with you, find a provider you trust and pursue your possibilities. It is free to search the online member directory at https://HolisticChamberOfCommerce.com, where we review references on our members before showcasing them in our directory.

In terms of physical health, I'm a big fan of not getting sick at all. I just don't have time. When I look at celebrities (they're so visible, it seems hard not to), I notice they don't seem to get sick either.

When you love what you do, including your work, you won't want a sick day (or even a mental-health day).

When you work long hours, you want to be healthy for your weekends and vacations.

How do we stay healthy, even when working crazy hours and living in crazy places?

Natalie Portman, Ellen DeGeneres, and Alicia Silverstone are all known for keeping a vegan diet. Katy Perry, Oprah Winfrey, and Sir Paul McCartney meditate.

There are so many options these days. What are the holistic wellness practices that can help you?

> Eat healthy foods; get nutrition counseling. Many people work with someone who can keep them on the straight and narrow when it comes to what they eat. Of course, you may already know that eating organic and natural fruit, veggies, and protein is better for you. If that's the case, take some advice from Nike, and "Just do it!"

You are what you eat. What are you eating?

> Exercise (with or without a physical trainer). If you're not getting the exercise you know is good for you, have you considered hiring a coach to keep you on target? Or for a more budget-friendly option, find a friend who also has a fitness goal and commit to each other. You can even share the cost of a physical trainer who is open to a two-for-one option or take a group class.

> Get a massage. Believe it or not, some people are still uncomfortable with this hands-on therapy. However, with stress well-documented as one of the four major factors leading to heart disease and stroke, a good massage can take care of your tension today, as well as your health tomorrow. Additionally, improved blood circulation is a benefit that increases overall physical conditioning, especially for aging adults.

> Visit a chiropractor. A chiropractor's years of training and understanding of skeletal structure can contribute to a routine, strong personal well-being program in a world where it is easy to get out of balance quickly. Chiropractic treatments have been shown to help with a wide range of health issues, from tendonitis, carpal tunnel syndrome, and headaches to problems such as constipation, obesity, and chronic fatigue. Some chiropractors even offer mobile services to clients.

> Try acupuncture. Long respected in Asia, acupuncture is known for its effectiveness in a variety of wellness areas. The National Institutes of Health (NIH) has begun to research this age-old healing method, and data supports its history. The California State Acupuncture Board confirms that licensed acupuncturists have had success with a variety of ailments, from allergy elimination to tinnitus.

> Consider colon hydrotherapy. Many people consider a colonic
way to detoxify the body and prepare for a new health regimen. Consider
this quote from Hippocrates: "The natural healing force within you is the
greatest force in getting well."

Perhaps you are emotionally constipated.

> Consider hypnotherapy. For anyone who knows what their health
goal is and how to reach it, yet hasn't taken the steps to get on track, a
hypnotherapist may be able to help shift the subconscious into gear. Most
commonly known for use in weight loss and smoking cessation programs,
hypnotherapy is also recognized as a powerful technique for reaching a
variety of personal and professional goals.

Of the other, more esoteric techniques you've probably heard of, such as
sound therapy and Reiki, it's harder to find statistical evidence of results.
Still, for those who accept anecdotal data, it's difficult to ignore the
potential benefits of these practices. Are they worth a try for you?

> Sound therapy is music with a therapeutic purpose. Usually performed
with drums or bowls, it can calm us in ways that nothing else can.
What's the value of being calm? When you're in the center of a storm,
whether family or business, it can make all the difference in the world. A
personalized concert, or sound bath, can soothe your soul.

Likewise, Reiki is an ancient art of healing rediscovered at the end of the
nineteenth century by Dr. Mikao Usui in Japan. It accelerates the body's
ability to heal physically by opening the mind and spirit to the source of
your physical concerns. Reiki is said to treat the whole person, rather than
just the symptoms, by tapping into "universal energy."

With all the options available for staying healthy these days, there's no need
for the world's health care crisis to become a personal one. If it has, it may
be time to open up to the alternatives.

Here are a few ideas to get you started:

PHYSICAL: BODY AND BEYOND

Start by looking for chiropractic, naturopathy, homeopathy, acupuncture, reflexology, massage therapy, nutrition counseling, fitness training (stress release!), cryotherapy, salt therapy (also called halotherapy), float therapy, and hyperbaric oxygen chambers.

THE CONNECTING TECHNIQUES: MIND AND BODY

Start by looking for yoga, hypnotherapy, dancing, neurofeedback, aromatherapy, flower essences, and essential oils therapy.

EMOTIONS AND ENERGY: NOT SO ESOTERIC

Start by looking for Reiki, sound healing, crystal bowls, emotional freedom technique (also known as EFT and tapping), access consciousness, Akashic records, sacred geometry, theta healing, and subtle energy.

If you are stalled on the road to better health, start by doing one thing. That's it—just one thing to jump-start your journey!

Consider these:

1. Drink an extra glass of water today.
2. Add lemon or lime to your water.
3. Drink your water from a wine glass to make it feel more special.
4. Add an unusual spice to one of your meals (for example, nutmeg on your oatmeal or turmeric in your tea).

TIME MANAGEMENT 101

It may be tempting to read this book in one sitting. It will be easy to read this book in one sitting. Perhaps you will do that.

Busy people, however, will always have something on the to-do list. If you are starting or maintaining a business that offers products and/or services to others, especially a cause-oriented business that is based on your desire to help others by providing value-based benefits, you may be busy.

When you have a lot that you want to accomplish, that's just the way it is. The first thing you'll need to do is come to terms with this concept.

There will always be something on your to-do list too.

The good news is that you are in fine company! I'm in the same boat. I'd be willing to bet that Oprah Winfrey is too, and Barack and Michelle Obama, Dr. Deepak Chopra, Dr. Andrew Weil, Stephen Colbert, Rachel Maddow, and a host of others.

The one thing that we all have in common is that there are only twenty-five hours in a day!

Making time for it all is one of our biggest challenges. It is also one of the reasons that stress is such a significant factor in our lives these days, especially with filtering through all the information that is available. We have news coming at us almost twenty-four/seven—online, on television, in print, and on the radio.

"Camille, how do you get it all done?"

I hear this question a lot, and here is the honest answer: I don't! Still, there are some keys that help keep my productivity on track so that I can achieve my goals more quickly. These keys can help you, too.

All too often, people who have plenty of money never seem to have enough time. Those who have plenty of time never seem to have enough money. My goal is to find a long-lasting balance between having the time to do what I want and the money to afford it.

My focus on holistic health and wellness depends on finding balance between the elements of living:

mind
body
soul
spirit
business
budget
planet

These include priorities in:

personal
professional
physical
financial
family

When it comes to time management, most people I know—from HCC members to fans, friends, and coaching clients—are stuck in one of three key areas:

> Personal (time for family, friends, and self)
> Professional (too much to do and not enough time to do it)
> Physical (no time for exercise and/or healthy eating)

Of course, money (or lack of it) also plays a role in balancing these factors. The more money you have, the more you can spend on wellness treatments, like massages (for personal stress relief), staff and consultants (to handle the work), or time available for exercising.

When you have more than enough money, if you are so inclined, you can also share it with others. It frees you up to choose how you want to spend your time: with family and friends, traveling, on your business, on hobbies, playing, and/or volunteering.

The tips shared here are the techniques I used every day in building the Holistic Chamber of Commerce, and they allowed me to keep expanding what is possible for our organization, taking our message of "healthier people on a healthier planet" to the rest of the world.

More important, these pointers can help you reach your transformational goals, whether they are for better health or a healthier business.

The HCC represents high-quality holistic and eco-friendly professionals and specialists so that we can reach and maintain life balance, leading to healthier and happier lives on a healthier planet, for ourselves *and* others. All our HCC professional members submit references, which we check, in order to ensure their commitment to quality and professionalism. Our professionals and specialists offer the products, services, and solutions mentioned here and can be found in a free search at HolisticChamberOfCommerce.com or by calling our office at 310-490-6862.

Important: When making health-related changes, it is recommended that you seek input from your primary-care doctor.

Do you have ongoing commitments (spouses, parents, children) to consider? Some people seemingly have more flexibility with their choices. Some of these tips will work for *you*; others will work better for your friend.

Use what works best for you, and skip the rest.

First, finding your focus makes a *huge* difference. Being able to quickly evaluate whether something is worth your time (or money) is critical to squeezing an extra hour into the day.

Have you hit a plateau? It's time to do something new and to power through!

One of the ongoing challenges in time management is determining which activities are building momentum and simply require patience and persistence and which tasks have become old ruts in which you are stuck.

If you are reading this book, you probably have a similar perspective to mine—that a holistic view of life and the world means appreciating and leveraging the interconnectedness of all of life and its elements. Aesop once said, "It is easy to be brave from a safe distance." I invite you to consider these ideas and find a way to be a bit braver, to close the distance between where you are today and where you really want to be.

You deserve to have more of what you really want by finding ways to manage your time and money more effectively, especially since having more time and/or money are usually what people want most. After all, isn't money just something that allows you to pay someone else to do what you don't want to do so you can spend that time doing something else?

These are practical tips that you can apply immediately, as well as food for thought about new time-management tools. You will find a combination of time-honored reminders (e.g., make a list), as well as suggestions for dealing with today's priorities. One example of this: check your junk mailbox or spam filter every day. Move anything important to your inbox, and delete the rest. If you let more than three days of junk sit there, it will become too overwhelming, and you won't be able to find the relevant stuff that slipped in by mistake. If there is too much in there already, *delete it all*. This will give you a clean slate and help you to create a fresh start of your own.

Warning: This material will probably be hazardous to your favorite excuses (I mean, "reasons") for saying no to activities that you don't have interest in. In other words, if you usually say, "I'm sick," "I can't afford it," or "I don't know how," when you want to get out of doing something, you won't be able to fall back on these anymore. You *will* be healthy and able to afford it. You'll be in a position to learn how or to hire someone who does.

On the other hand, you will be more comfortable saying yes when you do want to do something and saying no when you don't want to do it.

I have personally tried most of the things suggested here. They work in different ways for different people. This is just as relevant in business as it is in health care. Some people are allergic to peanuts, and others are not. Some people do best on Facebook and others prefer LinkedIn. That's why the Holistic Chamber of Commerce represents a variety of options.

Penicillin doesn't work for everyone. You need to find what works for you. I am simply sharing possibilities for you to consider so you can implement those that work best for you.

Your solutions will change over time. The tool or person that was helpful when you first started may not be a good fit as you move forward. Be open to finding new solutions as you make progress.

My personal disclaimer: If you haven't figured it out yet, I'm not perfect. I have an "all things in moderation, including moderation" lifestyle.

TIME, ENERGY, AND MONEY, HONEY!

These three elements affect how much money is available in your bank accounts and how much freedom you have to spend your time doing what you want to do.

Be healthy to be productive. The healthier you are (mind, body, spirit), the more you get done more quickly. That means that it's critical to invest in your overall health. I don't get sick (except when it's an excuse for avoiding someone or something that I don't want to deal with).

Eat well! Quality food equals quality energy. There are many ways to do this; find the best one for you. Whether you prefer a diet that is vegetarian, vegan, gluten-free, dairy-free, sugar-free, raw foods, ketogenic, omnivorous, Paleolithic, or a hybrid of these, with portion and quality control, one thing is clear: the more processed foods you eat, the more it will drag you down. Whole is better than processed. Organic is good. Fresh veggies are good. Bright colors are good. Green is good.

Exercise! Take that walk. Go for that jog. Get on your bike. Work out with a trainer who can help you keep up the routine that you want to start (but haven't yet). Dance. Take a yoga class. Exercise balances your body because too much energy can be as difficult to manage as too little energy. Really! Have you ever seen someone who is hyperactive? Have you ever met someone who is always bouncing from one idea from the next, never taking time to implement any of his or her ideas effectively?

Relax! Get a massage, especially with aromatherapy or essential oils. See an acupuncturist. Try sitting in a salt therapy room, hyperbaric oxygen chamber, or float chamber. Release physical and emotional constipation with colon hydrotherapy. Have a sound bath. Visit a ThetaHealing specialist or Reiki master.

Hydrate! Drink more water—quality water, even alkaline water. Get a filter.

Sleep! Get a good night's sleep (six to eight hours). Let yourself dream. Release the crap from the past day. Wake up to a new reality, with new possibilities and opportunities. Let new blessings take shape overnight.

Mind-body connections: All too often, the amount of energy we have and our ability to make solid, clear decisions has to do with our physical fitness *and* our mental and emotional health. On top of that, the more connection and stronger communication you have between your left and right brain hemispheres, the better you are at making balanced decisions more quickly and being able to take actions (including delegating the work) to reach the results you want.

Try hypnotherapy, yoga, acupuncture, or essential oils, as starting points. Consider also the wide variety of energy techniques that can help create a bridge from where you are today to where you want to be tomorrow and beyond. Meditate.

Delegate #1: Are you still trying to do it all on your own? Not only is that lonely, but it's ineffective. Successful entrepreneurs, even solopreneurs, have a team of advisers, consultants, and coaches who help them. Sometimes, we pay for services; other times, it's possible to arrange a trade.

Originally, when I first started the HCC, I did everything on my own (yes, from a living room "office"). As we grew, I hired a webmaster, a part-time assistant, an intern, and a bookkeeper. We've continued to grow! Yeah! So we keep hiring staff and consultants to handle the work involved.

Yes, it is scary. I had to deal with my commitment issues (committing to someone for his or her paycheck; that the work will continue, and the money will too), abandonment issues (what if it all goes away?), and my money issues (will I ever have enough?). If you feel like you are attached at the hip to your business, you probably are.

When people say, "Dig deeper," they are talking about finding the root of what is stopping you. It may be stuck in the seed of emotions from so far back that you don't even remember the original source of your present-day concern. All the same, it's still in your way.

Delegate #2: If personal time is your challenge, there are personal chefs, meal services, and housekeepers available to help with the basics. Don't know if you can afford it? Have you gotten a quote? Have you gotten several quotes? Just as an example, the HCC represents a variety of chefs, webmasters, and coaches. They all have different pricing packages.

Until you ask, you don't know if you can afford it. Odds are, once you find out how reasonable they are, you'll find the money.

Delegate #3: Learn to say yes when the right person offers to help you out. This will take letting go of your perfectionist tendencies or control issues and learning to trust others. Done right, you will now be able to say yes to new possibilities and opportunities that come your way.

Say *yes*: Do you wish you could say yes to the opportunities that come your way?

It took nine long years of focus for me, and I will always remember my 2019 birthday vacation. My mother had called in mid-November. She asked if I wanted to take a one-week trip to Baja California for my birthday in December. She offered to take me to an all-inclusive resort. All I had to do was pay for my airfare and any incidentals. Because of my initial efforts setting up a strong foundation of HCC procedures and hiring superb staff to handle the day-to-day details, I was able to accept this generous gift and join my mother in having a wonderful time.

Set yourself up today so you can say yes and transform your tomorrow.

Say it with me:

I am ready to say *yes*

to my dreams and desires!

...*ize* your space, mental and physical. Declutter regularly. Hire a professional organizer to help you get to a place where you can take it from there. Hire a housekeeper—even once a month is better (and more effective) than living and working in chaos.

Speaking of space, whenever you are on video, even if it is just as a watcher on a Zoom or other live onscreen webinar, look at what is *behind* you before you turn on the camera. If your kitchen, bedroom, or office is a mess behind you, everyone will see that. Is that really what you want to share?

Put your best foot forward. Following up on the above, once you've cleaned up your video background, consider making it actually work *for* you. You could add a few items that would support your business (if you have one) or otherwise make your presence pop.

Your background can speak for you:
when someone is deaf,
someone is watching without sound,
instead of your repeating yourself over and over,
when you are on a group call, where you might not have a chance to speak.

You could add
your book,
a sign with your logo,
toys to spread joy,
flowers (silk or fresh),
other books and items to inspire everyone else.

Avoid time-wasters (not to be confused with relaxation and rejuvenation). Excessive television, Solitaire, video games, or social media can get in the way.

What's excessive? Only you know the answer to that. Be honest with yourself.

Still, social media can also be an amazing tool for time management. I can reach five thousand friends and over ten thousand fans through Facebook.

Add in another network, and your social media reach is exponentially expanded. People pay attention and respond. One post can get the word out further and faster than any other method. Just don't lose track of time when connecting through social media.

Remember that a phone call may create a stronger result in some cases. Different goals and projects require different approaches.

Avoid Time-Wasters Special Note #1: Stop worrying. Science now shows that focusing on problems attracts problems. When you ask yourself, "What's the worst that could happen?," your mind is focused on all that can go wrong. Now, if you want to consider your challenges and look for solutions, that's fine. But worry itself is useless, and you don't have time for it. You'll be amazed by how much you can accomplish, once you put aside all your what-ifs. Whining about all that is going wrong is just another way to worry. Stop, and look for what is going right. Be thankful for the little wins. I once did a happy dance to celebrate a two-dollar royalty check. Really. Be thankful that your vision is bigger than your budget, and maybe your budget will grow big enough to cover the costs.

If you must, set your timer for one to two minutes, and allow yourself to write down your complaints. Then set your timer for twice as long (two to four minutes), and write down every idea that comes to mind for a new approach.

Where attention goes, energy flows.

There is *always* an option (even if you don't like it).

Time-Wasters Special Note #2: *Ask questions.* I work with a lot of people who spend time networking to find new clients and customers. If this is you, then save yourself (and others) some time by opening conversations with relevant questions that help you determine (1) if they are interested in what you offer, and (2) if they can afford (or are willing to pay) your prices.

There are billions of people in the world and, depending on where you live, probably over ten thousand in your community. When you find ways to work online and by phone, you'll have access to even more potential customers, clients, and patients. That's plenty of people who could need you and want what you offer. Don't waste time on those who don't. Go find the people who want what you sell, can afford it, and are willing to pay for it.

Asking questions first, before launching into the miraculous healing powers of your special product/service, will help you spend time with those who appreciate and value you and what you do.

Happily, asking questions will create a conversation that not only helps you determine how best to communicate what you do but also helps your potential new clients or customers to see the value of what you offer. Subsequently, they just might purchase your product or service or say yes to being on your email list.

After exchanging names, some good questions to start with include:

1. What brought you to this meeting/event?
2. Do you have any goals this month/year?
3. What is your favorite thing about your life right now?

When you listen to their answers, you'll know whether it makes sense to continue this conversation or not.

Whatever happens, it is important to reach out on social media and connect there. By staying connected, it will be easier for them to find you when they (or someone they know) needs or wants your product/service.

Rest and relaxation: Instead of wasting time in all the ways that are possible, schedule an appointment with a holistic healing professional. Whether it's massage, yoga, sound therapy, Reiki, meditation, floating, or some combination, one hour can provide much more benefit than an hour of junk.

Plan: Yes, boys and girls, I keep a few lists and cross things off. At least once a week, I pull all my lists together and consolidate, rearranging priorities and removing those tasks that aren't significant. If you don't like making physical lists on paper, there are plenty of productivity apps for your phone or computer. Use whatever works for you.

A list is not a plan. It is an approach to planning. It is an element of a good plan. It is helpful, but it is not the entire thing.

If thinking in terms of long-term goals is a challenge for you (as it has been for me), consider setting up a variety of lists for the different items needed to reach your long-term goals. You could also set it up like a table of contents (yes, the kind used for a book) but in a time line sort of way. Chapter 1 would be either goal 1 (your first step) or week 1. Subsequent "chapters" would show the little goals that you want to accomplish weekly. You could set this up with your chapters as days or months.

When you are working on a large project or business goal, creating a visual guide that you can keep referring back to can be very beneficial.

Focus your time: "One thing at a time" usually means getting that one thing done more quickly and then accomplishing more things over time.

It's definitely a domino effect. You might call it a ripple effect or a butterfly effect, but they're all the same concept—one action can change the future, no matter how small.

Say, "Yes, thank you!" Accept and appreciate offers of assistance. If you are still saying, "No thanks. I can do it all myself," no wonder you are overwhelmed. If people aren't offering anymore, it may be that they have learned you don't want their help. You may need to ask.

Say, "No, I'm not available." If you are still saying yes to things you don't want to do or don't have time for or that don't fit in with your current priorities, then no wonder you don't have time for your vision and your life. You may have to practice saying no. I certainly did. (More on this topic later.)

IT'S YOUR PATH, YOUR JOURNEY

You may be tempted to compare yourself to others. Resist this temptation. Interview others for information, and then make your own choices. Many successful people have multiple college degrees, and many others have none at all. Some businesses use websites, Facebook, Twitter, and the like, and other successful businesses don't. It's your business. Today's stress is just a choice. Good decisions and timely implementation build businesses that succeed. In the long run, it's the cumulative effect that matters most.

Being leads to doing; doing leads to being. These two concepts (*being* and *doing*) go hand in hand. Visualization without action won't bring results, and likewise, action without contemplation (or meditation or stillness) will not bring love, peace, joy, or serenity, which are among the best elements of overall success.

Breathe deeply. Proceed with calm and consideration. Take time for a breath of fresh air to clear your mind and soothe your soul. Often, this moment of stillness can help you determine the best course of action so that you will receive the results you seek.

Focus on solutions, not problems. When you find yourself thinking about a problem, shift your attention to the options you have to solve it. Embrace the challenge.

Network with solution-oriented professionals. We all face many of the same types of challenges. By collaborating, we can share ideas and insights to help us find the solutions that will work for us. As we each become stronger, we *all* become stronger. Likewise, as we all become more successful, we *each* become more successful.

Live in the present with an eye to the future. You may be inclined to revisit your past story, and certainly, it can be useful to learn from it (particularly past mistakes), but don't dwell on the past. It is more productive to focus your time and your energy on the here and now with a vision toward reaching your future goals.

Enjoy this moment. You may never pass this way again. Every day and each experience is unique unto itself. Seize the day, and appreciate each moment as it comes.

The best time to plant a tree was twenty years ago. The next best time to plant a tree is today. You've probably heard that before. Whatever it is that you are putting off, start now. Remember, though, that it takes time to grow a tree. Your work will pay off but maybe not today. Take timely action, and then practice patience and persistence.

There is oneness and duality in the approach of action and stillness. They work hand in hand. Follow up with a lead today, and wait a few days for that lead to respond. If needed, follow up again later.

People need you and your gift. Please remember that your personal blend of compassion, goodness, and positive perspective is invaluable. You are one of a kind.

Please don't hide your light. Let your light shine! The world needs you.

Keep a positive tone of voice. Speak in a strong, confident, comfortable, and warm tone (not soft and weak or hard and cold). Your inner emotions will affect your tone of voice. If you are feeling desperate, nervous, or worried, you may be perceived as uptight, rather than relaxed. Take a deep breath, and think positive thoughts.

Words matter. Don't bang on it; massage the details instead. What words are you using? Can you flip them for a positive focus? Practice phrasing things positively.

Believe in yourself. Some will question you, and others will discourage you. Actor Sigourney Weaver was told in drama school that she would never make it in the business. Aren't we glad she didn't let those voices defeat her? Be open to constructive criticism, while being aware that some comments are not relevant for you.

Is terminology important? Does it matter what words you use? What matters most is that you are comfortable with how you describe what you do *and* that the person with whom you are in a conversation understands what you are saying. If they don't, they may not ask.

Practice your pitch so that you are at ease with it. Be aware of your audience and, as often as possible, use terminology that fits them. For example, in communicating with audiences of holistic practitioners vs. corporate business people vs. first responders, you would (and should) use different and varied terminology.

Does it matter what you wear?

Your clothes are your words when you are not speaking. People, unless they are blind, usually see you before they hear you. They start making judgments based on the visual. Are you professional? Trustworthy? Educated in your field of practice? Knowledgeable? Attentive?

If I'm going to spend my money with you, especially for a service related to my physical health or the health of my business and budget, and we meet in person or via a visual format (such as Zoom), you should look the part.

Otherwise, I'm back to Google and looking for someone else. There is always someone else.

People may even be willing to spend more money on someone else, once they see you as the low-budget option. If it will make a difference in how people respond to you, if they will pay more attention to the important message you have, it is worth your time and money to consider your audience (whether it's one or one hundred or one thousand-plus), and dress appropriately.

Be clear. Where do you spend your time, money, and energy? Many holistic entrepreneurs market too much at once and try too hard to get to the endgame when they have just met someone. Don't rush it! It is more effective to first get potential customers interested and engaged before marketing your services. Put yourself in their shoes. Consider your own response when you meet someone, and they launch into their full pitch right away. Are you likely to buy, or do you start thinking of how best to get away?

Don't make your decisions in a vacuum. Consulting solely with your best buddies and workmates is not the best approach. Even your family may not be the best source of input on your new project or business. Get with a group of people you know and some that you don't. Brainstorm together. Introduce ideas and ask for input. Varying and divergent perspectives will broaden your horizons and help you find the best solutions for you.

Find technology that works for you. Today, there are many high-tech applications that are available for free or at a low cost. Find what works for you and use it. This can save you time and money and, more importantly, can result in a much more successful and satisfying enterprise.

When choosing technology services, or any product/service, remember that sometimes you get what you pay for and sometimes you don't. If it is free, it may be a waste of your time. It may be that it's not user-friendly and you don't use it. On the other hand, some free tools are very helpful. Likewise, the most expensive option may not be the best choice for you.

PARTNERING

You can't partner with just anyone, and you can't partner with everyone. Working alone has its own features—some positive and some not so much. Though you may find the unilateral control of working by yourself appealing, you will lose out on the benefit of additional talents and having another point of view. A compatible partnership will often accomplish more than one can achieve alone—and more quickly.

But partnering with someone also has challenges. It can be complex, with a steep learning curve on how best to work together productively. And working with the *wrong* partner can be counterproductive, sapping you of good energy. Anyone who has ever been divorced is likely to point out that you can get far more done alone (and enjoy it more) than if you are struggling to make things work with the wrong partner.

Remember that even if one partner is more visible, someone else is likely handling the background details. Warren Buffett has Charlie Munger. Google was started by Larry Page and Sergey Brin. Oprah Winfrey and Gayle King have been together, side by side, for decades. Patience in choosing a partner is more than a virtue here. It just might be the difference between success and failure.

Choose carefully.

THE WHOLE IS GREATER THAN
THE SUM OF ITS PARTS

Collaborative opportunities can help you maximize value for both your time and money. Joining an organization like the Holistic Chamber of Commerce (or Toastmasters, Rotary Club, Business Networking International [BNI], or any number of similar organizations) allows you to benefit from other members' work on marketing and promotions, as well as providing easy access to a group of like-minded professionals and business owners. It's pretty much the same principle as joining Costco for the prices they can negotiate, based on their numbers. Likewise, Starbucks is more successful, in part, because of the number of their locations. They can get better prices and provide better employee benefits, thanks to the numbers involved. If you are an economics major, you might call it *economies of scale*.

In the jungle, some cats travel together, while others prefer the solitary path. In business, there are times when solitude can help you focus on the task at hand and other times when collaboration is most helpful.

Be flexible, and, like a cat, you will always land on your feet. Remember that the biggest cats—lions—travel together. If you are always trying to do everything on your own, it will take more work, time, and energy.

IS YOUR PASSION HELPING OR HURTING?

Is your passion helping or hurting?

Note 1: Do you know someone who is so excited about what they have to share (product, service, or idea/opinion) that they end up interrupting (instead of listening). Is that you? Always be a good and attentive listener. When you listen well, more people are likely to listen to you when you have something to say. They will spend more time with you and, when ready, call you first. No one likes a pushy person.

Is your passion helping or hurting?

Note 2: Some passionate people feel that who they are on the inside is more important than their outward appearance. On the whole, it is. It is understandable that if you feel that your appearance and style of dress is not reflective of your inner self, it's not important, and you may pay little attention to those details. However, your potential customer is looking at you and comparing you to the competition. If you can improve your chances of succeeding in your business with a little more attention to appearance, isn't it worth the effort? What you look like (yes, your image) matters. For many people, the old Flip Wilson saying still holds: "What you see is what you get." Make sure they see the you that shows all of you in the best light. This is not masquerading. It is putting your best foot forward. It says, "I care about doing my best for you."

This doesn't mean you have to dress like everyone else. Today we are blessed with a variety of online style guides and options. Consider creating a style of your own that balances professionalism with creativity.

Note 3: Obviously, you are a big fan of your work and believe strongly in what you do. Sometimes, though, passionate business owners will use terminology in their writings and presentations that makes no sense to the potential customer. For example, if your business card reads "NAET," it is unlikely that most people will know that you are an expert in

Allergy Elimination Technique. Seek ways to communicate usir
straightforward, and easily understandable terms. An abbreviation that is
unknown to the person reading it may not help you (or them) at all.

More letters after your name does not automatically help. Think of me as
your potential customer. If I don't know what the letters stand for, I might
not care. It won't make a difference and could actually get in the way, as it
distracts from the product/service that you want me to purchase.

Listing too many therapeutic modalities on your business card does not
automatically help you. In fact, it may hurt. If you have listed too many
specialties, I (your potential customer) see two challenges:

1. I will wonder if you are any good at any of them.
2. More words on an already small business card means less room
    and smaller font size, both of which make for difficult reading.

On your card, show the techniques in which you are strongest, and save
the extensive listing for your website or on an informative sign posted in
your place of business. With a long list, consider grouping specialties under
subgroups so potential customers are not overwhelmed.

What are some ways in which your passion helps you? Are there any ways
in which your passion gets in the way?

Write about it here:

BE ABLE TO ADAPT YOUR APPROACH

Blessed are the flexible, for they shall not get bent out of shape! This does *not* mean that you are always changing your principles and values. It means that you'll want to be agile and adaptable in your approach. Technology is changing almost every day, and this trait can be the key to an effective business-building strategy.

Furthermore, everyone you meet is a different person, with a variety of preferences that most likely differ from those of the last person you met. What worked yesterday may not work today. Depending on funding, you may be responsible for everything from sales to administration to cleaning house and whatever. Being flexible helps you adjust quickly to the new situations and circumstances that are sure to come up.

Is there a way in which you could be more flexible or adaptable? Is there an area where you have been too rigid and have held yourself back from the rewards you seek?

Write about it here:

STAY HEALTHY, HAPPY, AND (RELATIVELY) STRESS-FREE!

Whatever you are selling, most people are interested in buying something that will help them have more of what they want... health, happiness, freedom, time, money, or success-- in all the ways that people define it. Visualize and project the image of one who already is healthy, happy, stress-free, and successful. If you don't, then why would your potential customers believe that your service or product will work for them? Be your own best advertisement. As an example, I know a medical intuitive who says that he can tell me what is holding me back from success. The problem is, I only hear from him when he's not succeeding, when he is trying hard to sell me his service. It's a matter of credibility. The coaches and healing professionals that I hire have something that I want, and it shows.

A person is much more likely to accept advice about how to succeed from someone who demonstrates success. Perception matters.

Your body is your temple: Holistic professionals sometimes forget to work with other holistic professionals when they are busy building their businesses from scratch. I know because it was a personal weakness of mine.

Take your own advice: Get a massage, an acupuncture treatment, or a chiropractic adjustment—anything that improves your health and/or state of mind. Go see a Reiki master. Take care of yourself. If you are used to eating a particular diet or drinking a specific nutritional supplement, keep it up. Your health is of vital importance, not only for conducting a successful business but for your own personal well-being.

How do you sell an intangible?: Holistic professionals often deal with the intangible. Many of the products and services they provide are designed to be preventive and protective (for the person or for the planet), rather than an immediate commodity or a tangible item that the customer walks away with. For example, when I go to an attorney, I walk away with a contract or a specific course of action to take, given a set of circumstances. It is tangible. Though a supplement designed to keep me healthy is a real product that I purchase and consume, it is not exactly the same because how do we measure what *didn't* happen—I didn't get sick? One way is to remind customers how well they are doing by what is *not* happening; for instance, not getting sick, not gaining weight, not losing their tempers in reaction to a trigger that used to bother them.

The placebo effect: Interestingly, placebos (pills designed to resemble an active medication but typically made of starch or sugar) can have the same effect as the real prescription. This indicates that people are so comfortable with a tangible—in this case, a pill—that it works in the healing process whether it has any medicinal value or not. Behold the power of our mind/body connection! Since we are in the business of healing, whether it is physical, emotional, or stress-related, we should be mindful of the benefits of placebos, as well as the value of our primary service.

When people are healed, they feel better. They pay for the result and are happy with it.

Learn from experience (yours and that of other people): It would be great if we all learned the easy way—by being told what to do and when to do it. History shows us, however, that the most valuable lessons are learned through experience (the school of hard knocks). For that matter, some of us don't listen when someone tells us what works and what doesn't. We think to ourselves, *I can do it my way. I'll show them a better way. That's what they think*, and any number of other reasons for not taking advice.

What worked for someone else may not work for you. Still, consider that there is something to learn from other people's mistakes (because you might not live long enough to make those mistakes yourself). They say that with age comes wisdom, but sometimes, age comes all by itself. Let that not be true of you.

Coaches and role models (the laws of karma and attraction): Other than learning through formal training and personal experience, there are two good ways to become skilled at designing, developing, and maintaining your business:

1. Work with a coach who can help you apply lessons directly to your specific needs and circumstances.
2. Choose a quality role model, watch what that person does, and ask questions.

If you select either (or both) of these options, remember the laws of karma and attraction. According to karma, we receive what we give. The law of attraction is similar, as like attracts like. If you are unwilling to pay your coach or teacher for the valuable expertise that person offers, you may find yourself surrounded by others who don't want to pay you for the services and/or products that you offer. If all your potential clients and customers ask for freebies and discounts, look at your negotiations and interactions to see how often you seek freebies and discounts.

Figure out what you can afford, and start paying for it, and you will attract people who will pay you.

to say no: Periodically, people complain to me. Usually, it's about something that they paid too much for but they couldn't get a refund. They are irritated with themselves and want to blame the other person. Here is a list of ways to say no in the first place:

"No."
"Thanks, but no thanks."
"Not right now."
"Maybe next month."
"Call me next month."
"It's not a good fit."
"I'll consider it for the future."
"I'd love to, but I don't have time right now."
"I'd love to, but my money is all tied up in other investments."

Say yes when it makes sense for you. The rest of the time, consider saying no (see above) so you can focus on *your* priorities instead of on someone else's.

Respond promptly to all customer and potential-customer communications. I know some professionals who, due to a seemingly overwhelming workload or the drudgery of dealing with technology, turn off their phones and/or avoid their emails for several days at a time. Now consider your own reaction to a business that doesn't return a phone call or reply to an email within a reasonable period of time (say, twenty-four to forty-eight hours). Would you start looking for a different source? I know I would.

Take a lesson from Starbucks: Why do we pay so much for coffee these days? Why do you think Starbucks is so successful? It is the consistent, dependable service; taste of the drinks; and fast delivery. People know what they're going to get, how much it's going to cost, and how quickly they're going to get it—every single time. That is something we are willing to pay for.

Reliability—the hallmark of a successful business: It is human nature to value a consistent and reliable relationship, whether in our personal lives or in our business affairs. Your customers want a relationship they can count on. They want to know that your product or service will be available when they need it. Especially concerning our health and the well-being of our money, we want to know that our key providers (you) will be available when we need them.

Be able, available, and ready to roll. If I can't reach you, or you can't deliver in a timely way, I'll get it somewhere else. Once I go somewhere else, I may not return to you.

If you are a healing professional, this is all the more important. When I'm concerned about my health, I want a service provider (doctor, adviser, chiropractor, acupuncturist, naturopath, homeopath) who I know will be there when an issue comes up. If you seem undependable, your potential clients probably will look for someone else.

Practical note: You must also be reasonably easy to access. If your voice mail is full and your patients or clients can't leave a message, how can they tell you what is wrong? How will you know if it's important for them to get advice right away or if it's something that can wait? If it were me, I'd look for someone else who is available to answer my questions when needed; someone I can trust to be responsive when it's important.

Change happens when we choose it. The solution of three years ago may not be a good fit for today. This includes people in your inner circle and on your core team. Frankly, this is key to your ongoing transformation. Think of it like driving a car—driving a Hyundai Sonata is not like driving a Porsche 911, and it's altogether different from riding in the back of a limousine. Likewise, running a business with three employees and 150 customers is distinct from one with thirty employees and fifteen thousand customers. The people you associate with are likely different in all these cases as well. Your transformation means ongoing change in the people you hang out with, as well as the ways you spend your time. What choices are you making? What changes make sense for you now?

Letting go is an ongoing process.

Receiving more is an ongoing process.

IS IT A SPLINTER?

If you have a problem, it's useful to treat it like a splinter, and consider your options for how to handle it.

Do you need to pull it out now, or will it work itself out on its own?

Some splinters fester and become infected. Others go quietly away. When a problem comes up, take a second to consider whether you need to deal with it or if it will go away on its own.

Often, problems with other people are about attention. If you don't pay attention to those people and the problems they are creating, they will go away. Don't let them distract you from your primary goals.

When you can, wait until the next day to respond.

Do you have any problems on your plate right now? Is it a splinter that you should deal with or one that will go away when you ignore it?

Write about it here:

WHAT IS YOUR UNDERLYING ASSUMPTION?

If you assume that people can't afford what you offer or sell, then you are not helping anyone. What if they have plenty of money and truly would benefit from your expertise? If you are making assumptions about other people based on *your* experience, it's time to reconsider. Others come from different backgrounds. Their issues, concerns, needs, and *budget* are not the same as yours. Give them the opportunity to hear about what you offer and to purchase your product(s) and/or service(s).

How many times has someone said, "No, I can't afford it," and then you see them shopping in Whole Foods or making a large purchase at Costco? They have the money. They just need time to realize that spending it on your product/service will help them. If you keep giving it away for free, they will keep accepting your handouts.

Don't let the struggle define you. If you do, you can get stuck there. Move to easy and effortless by releasing the struggle and opening yourself to receiving abundance, wealth, and money with grace and ease.

It is only one step from climbing the mountain to being at the top of it. Allow yourself to take that step and live at the top!

Is there an area where you might be making assumptions that hold you back? Can you be open to other possibilities?

Write about it here:

CHOOSING CHANGE

Change happens when we choose it. What choices are you making?

What changes can you start making now that will create more of what you want in the future?

Write about them here:

SHORT TERM VS. LONG TERM

In terms of branding and marketing and sales, will your choices support the overall image of your focus? Will your marketing materials and prices only attract those who are looking for freebies, or will they attract those who can afford your products or services *and* are willing to pay for them? Groupon is effective for some businesses but not necessarily yours. If you sell a ton of stuff for a super-low price, you will attract customers who will only buy at that super-low price. Will they keep coming back at your regular prices? Would it be better to spend your money looking for customers who can afford your regular prices and are willing to pay them? Where are you looking, and how are you communicating your value?

Answer these questions, and shift your focus accordingly; then you will find your business growing bigger and better all the time.

ROLE MODELS

Special thanks to my role models. I appreciate you for leading the way so that we all can see a bright future for everyone. Note that the following list is based on where I am today—those who influence me now. By the time you read this book, it may have changed.

In alphabetical order, they are:

Alicia Keys
Aretha Franklin
Barbara Corcoran
Bonnie Raitt
Carol Burnett
Daymond John
Dr. Andrew Weil
Dr. Deepak Chopra
Dr. Mehmet Oz
The Jonas Brothers
Lucille Ball
Napoleon Hill
Nelson Mandela
Oprah Winfrey
Robin Williams
Stephen Colbert
Taylor Swift

What do my role models have in common (other than me)?

They are all making money *and* making a difference by focusing on what they love and what they are good at (or they did when they were alive). They are creative! For some of them, it's sharing joy and music with the rest of the world. For others, their purpose is in increasing awareness and education in a certain aspect of life (e.g., health).

I've heard some people say things like, "Oh, I wouldn't want to get my hands dirty by charging money or doing anything sales-y."

Really? How can people find you to get the help you offer? Don't you need to do some marketing and/or advertising? If people can't find you, then you're not helping anyone. If you're not charging, and people aren't taking you seriously, it's the same effect. Plus, if you're not making money, you'll eventually have to get another job to pay your basic bills. Then you won't have time or availability to help anyone else.

When you find a way to have healthy money by charging fair prices for your products/services, you help yourself *and* everyone else.

Who are your role models? Why did you choose them?

Write about them here:

GETTING OUT OF YOUR OWN WAY

Avoid issues that lead to public controversy, *unless* your business is specific to that controversy.

Strong opinions, especially on some hot-button issues, will turn off potential customers, clients, and patients *before* they have a chance to meet you. You want to meet them, and you want them to meet you so you can create bridges with each other.

Because I run the Holistic Chamber of Commerce, it's clear to me that my priority is to open doors. I don't want to push people away. I want to attract attention to our high-quality HCC members and the products and services they offer. That means talking more about possibilities, opportunities, and solutions than about problems.

Do you have any strong opinions that might be getting in your way? What are they? Can you hold your tongue in public so that more people can get to know you (and your products and services) first?

Write about it here:

SHORT-TERM RESULTS VS. LONG-TERM CONSEQUENCES

I have bills to pay. So do you. They are due when they are due. We may get to delay the payment for a little while by using a credit card or borrowing from a friend. Still, bills eventually need to be paid. You help your finances if you choose to live within your means. Running a business can be stressful enough; there's no need to add to it. As your business grows, you can reap your rewards.

Some things are just set in time. Holidays, for example, happen when they happen. They're predictable. You may not want to celebrate or refrain from work on that day, but many people do, whether you do or not.

When you schedule a special event (first-ever conference, anyone?), it's for a specific day and time. People will show up, then and there, or they won't. If they don't, then they missed it.

Then there are long-term consequences. What happens, for better or worse (down the road), is based on actions taken (or not taken) today.

The oil spill in the Gulf of Mexico caused by BP Energy is one example. The choices made by the leadership teams of Enron and Arthur Andersen are another.

Likewise, you can take important actions today that will move you forward in reaching your goals and creating the results that you want. These actions may or may not show up in results today. They will still make a key difference for your future, whether it's tomorrow, next week, next month, or even next year.

It took six years to get the Holistic Chamber of Commerce to the point where I felt comfortable taking a long holiday weekend. Some of my early decisions got this organization to this point so quickly. At the time, it didn't feel quick at all. It felt like long hours every day.

Finding the balance between oneness and duality comes up often in building a business:

Short-term results; long-term consequences
Stillness/meditation/visualization; implementation/action
Patience/waiting; following up

Beware of going in circles; you'll never move forward. Ask yourself where you want to go, where you want to be. Raise your eyes, and keep them on the prize. It will help you put your feet on the right path.

HIGH-PRICED AGREEMENTS

If you purchase something with a high price tag (coaching services, website/technology, or something similar), consider setting up a payment agreement with a refund policy. Put your agreement in writing.

Especially if it is nonrefundable, which is sometimes the case with coaches, see if you can pay 50 percent to start and the remaining 50 percent at the midway point.

For a website, offer 50 percent as a down payment, and set up delivery dates contingent on agreed-upon performance measures for the remaining payments. For example, 50 percent to start, 25 percent at the halfway point, and the remaining 25 percent when the project is completed. Be sure to get key items included. With your website, you should get the passwords so that you can log in and update basic text on your own. If you can't get that, find someone else.

PERSONAL AND PROFESSIONAL

WHERE THE RUBBER MEETS THE ROAD

Very often, especially for entrepreneurs, our personal issues and professional concerns intersect.

It is easiest to understand this when we consider that the stress of the workday is often the first thing we talk about when we get home and that stress from home in the morning influences our early interactions on any given day.

TRUST ISSUES

When the Holistic Chamber of Commerce started growing, my trust issues were the first ones that got in my way, and had to be "healed" to allow for expansion.

It took trust to bring on a chapter president that I had never met in person.

It took trust to hire staff and consultants, and let them do their jobs.

Unfortunately, my baggage from when I was young was getting in the way because I didn't trust anyone to help. I also didn't trust myself to make good decisions.

After a few sessions with several members, I was able to forgive myself and others, and trust people around me now to keep their commitments even though people from my past had let me down.

Is a lack of trust in others blocking you from your success? Is a lack of trust *in yourself* in your way?

Write about it here:

RUFFLED FEATHERS

One of the social media posts that ruffles my feathers has gotten me to write this essay that is *meant* to ruffle your feathers.

Don't we all know what money won't buy? It won't buy love, peace, calm, joy, happiness, respect, character, integrity, truth, honesty. Whatever.

Some people need a reminder of what money will buy: food, rent/mortgage, utilities, clothing, gas for the car (not to mention the car) and/or transportation, child care, a massage, health care and wellness treatments, travel/recreation, staff and consultants, and upgraded technology, among other things.

Money is neutral. It can be used to positive, negative, or indifferent ends. With good choices, money can do a lot of good.

That's why I preach the "get good at business" gospel. I want positive people, who are doing beneficial things, to have more money so they can multiply the good they already are doing.

If you think you have to ignore your values in order to earn a paycheck, I'm happy to share that I know a growing number of people who are making more money by learning how to build a business in alignment with their values. Others are working for successful companies that share their values.

It's not just the big businesses, like Whole Foods Markets, Trader Joe's, Patagonia, Ben & Jerry's, Annie's Organics, Arbonne International, Nikken, Melaleuca, SendOutCards, and so on. Solopreneurs and health and wellness professionals are creating success as well. They are acupuncturists, chiropractors, hypnotherapists, essential oils experts, massage therapists, and more.

Here's the deal, though. If you pay full price at a big chain grocery store and then negotiate with your friend for a discount, you are supporting a corporation while undermining your friend.

Let's support all—friends and family and small and big businesses alike. All have value and offer products and services that make our lives better.

EVOLVING THE WORLD

The holistic approach to health, lifestyle, and business is that when you want to evolve the world, you have to invite everybody with an open heart and mind.

Frequently, this means loving more and judging less.

Where are you judging yourself? Can you forgive yourself in those areas? For not knowing then what you know now? For allowing your emotions to railroad your intentions?

Who else are you judging? Can you forgive them? Then, either keep the relationship in a more caring way, or let the relationship go.

Can you love yourself more? What can you do now to show yourself more love?

Can you love others more? What can you do for others that will show them your heart is open?

Finding compassion and forgiveness for each other, while still taking care of ourselves, is an important balance.

If we can't learn to love each other, how can we help the rest of the world to love?

Can you find ways to take care of yourself without blaming the other person for his or her "bad" behavior?

Write about it here:

SHREWD AS SNAKES

Jesus says, "Be as shrewd as serpents and as innocent as doves" (Matthew 10:16).

We can be smart. There is nothing in the Bible or any other holy and sacred manuscript that calls you, me, or anyone else to stupidity or poverty. At the same time, we are not called to gluttony and greed either.

We *are* called to abundance and prosperity, while not harming others and being given guidance on fairness and generosity.

Balance, see?

This brings us back to the question and concept of oneness and duality and how it is possible to embody seeming opposites within oneself.

THE MYTH OF PRODUCTIVITY

Somehow, much of the world seems to see productivity as a primary factor in super-success stories. I suppose that it's possible, depending on how you define productivity.

Don't get me wrong; I've worked hard to get where I am today. There have been days, weeks, months, and years that were all work and no play. This is not necessarily productivity, though it seemed like it at the time. Oprah Winfrey had a 6:00 a.m. wake-up time every day for decades. I agree with Daymond John when he writes about the value of a *Rise and Grind* work ethic of "grit, persistence and good old-fashioned hard work."

Still, you want to get to a stage where it's not all work, all the time; where you can take time off to breathe, relax, stretch, and—yes—even vacation.

To get the results and rewards you seek, there likely will be a period when you invest your time and money in setting up a strong and solid foundation. Depending on your vision and mission, that time may be longer than you expected when you started. It was for me.

Still, the goal likely will get to a point where you have financial freedom, which is to say, the freedom to spend your time as you would like because you have enough money in the bank to pay your bills. There is no debt, and you can easily say, "I am financially free." What a beautiful day that will be for you, as it is for me now.

Productivity, though, doesn't mean that you are always at work. It means that when you are working, you are creating results that lead to rewards—financial and otherwise—and to accomplishing the goals you've set for yourself and your company.

Productivity leaves you plenty of free time for family, fun, play, or whatever else you would like to do. Perhaps you would like drive race cars, paint, do yoga, swim, or even write a book, just for the fun of it. Perhaps you want to dance or act or play an instrument. What do you want to do?

Being productive means that you accomplish more in the same amount of time or less.

The biggest and best aha moments often come from asking powerful questions that open creative conversations for greater growth in key areas.

This active exploration of available or potential options often leads to transformation, in terms of the windows and doors opening up for you.

If you are in business, either as a solopreneur or developing a larger enterprise, this section is for you!

DEALING WITH CHANGE

This book is about transformation, and that is *all* about change. Even so, it is worth covering this topic in its own section.

When change happens—unwanted or wanted, expected or unexpected—as it did in March 2020 in the United States, we get to choose our response.

We are all in different situations. Recognize that. Some people may be thrilled with the chance to change; others, not so much.

Do not make assumptions. Some changes will be for the better; others will require that you explore what shifts make sense for you and take a fresh approach.

Do you look at the problems or the possibilities? To find your solutions, keep your eyes and ears open to suggestions and ideas that can help. While you may not feel like you have control over all the factors, you can always look for new opportunities that may arise.

Be open to exploring! What will work for one person may or may not work for another.

QUESTIONS TO START THIS CONVERSATION

1. What is important *now*? (Not yesterday. Old priorities may no longer apply.)
2. How is this good for me? Where is my silver lining?
3. What possibilities and opportunities are available now? Am I missing anything?
4. What is my vision for my future?

IDEAS TO CONSIDER

Keep in mind that these may not apply to you, depending on your individual circumstances. Look for *your* opportunities.

- Early reports during the COVID-19 situation indicated an increase in people wanting home births. For a midwife comfortable with a certain level of risk, this could be good. For a medical or bodywork professional, home/office visits might also be an option in a case like this.
- Other professionals found this to be an opportunity to learn a new skill so that they could provide services using online technology for video conferencing. One HCC member who specializes in senior fitness already had discovered that she could provide coaching via Zoom. Explore your possibilities!
- Do you have more time on your hands? Send thank-you notes to your customers. Write your book. Plan the next stage of your life. Create (or update) your website and social media.

CAN'T SEE THE FOREST FOR THE TREES?

- It's too easy to get stuck in one view (the forest) or another (the trees). Take this time to pull back or focus in, and look at your business from a new perspective.
- Read some of the articles available at HolisticChamberofCommerce. com. Covering a range of subjects—from holistic health care to your personal purpose to creating a healthy bottom line—these essays can bring your attention to items that could simplify your ongoing efforts for more success.

TIME MANAGEMENT FOR *YOU*

In talking with HCC members, I've seen two core areas of challenge:

1. Finding and keeping a steady stream of customers, clients, and patients.
2. Having the time to handle both the services end for orders and appointments *and* taking care of the administrative concerns (financial record-keeping, website maintenance, marketing, etc.).

A thorough examination of your time management concerns should encompass all aspects of your life. Be sure to include personal and professional to-do items.

Figuring out what works best for you will help you get and stay richer, emotionally and financially.

Professional: job (if you have one); business; email; blog posts; social media; seeing clients, customers, patients; phone calls; video creation; ordering supplies; bookkeeping; website updates; preparing for speaking gigs; planning and promoting events; networking meetings.

Personal: children; family; friends; laundry; housekeeping; meals; self-care; hobbies.

Sleep.

QUESTIONS TO START THIS CONVERSATION

1. What is the source of your primary income, and how much time does it take on an average day?
2. What are the three activities that require the largest amount of your time?

3. What do you do yourself, and what can you delegate? Delegate to your children (if an age-appropriate task), spouse (or other relatives, if willing, and it works for you), volunteers/interns, and/ or paid help, like consultants and staff.
4. Do you have or can you hire employees (full-time or part-time) or any regular contractors (housekeeper, webmaster, bookkeeper, etc.)?
5. What tools do you use for saving time and/or money? Saving money allows you to have more money for spending on time-saving tools, including people to work for you or systems that simplify your work.

TAME YOUR EMAIL

1. Empty your spam folder of *everything*. It's just weighing you down. Then, check it once per day. Keep what you need, and delete the rest.
2. Daily, delete the items that you don't need, and handle the items you do. Save relevant items in an "action" folder or folders for specific projects.
3. Limit the number of email addresses you have to check. It makes sense to have a personal email that is separate from your professional email. You may even have an additional email address for a specific purpose, especially if you don't have to check it every day. More than three or four email addresses is cumbersome and wastes your time.

TAME YOUR SCHEDULE

The thing that takes you eight hours and leaves you stressed probably takes a professional eight minutes, *and* you will be much more effective in everything else you do.

1. What do you most dislike doing that you could easily delegate to someone else?

2. What is the item that has been sitting on your to-do list the longest or gets you stressed every time you think about it? Is it housekeeping, the website, or bookkeeping? It is relatively easy to find help with any of these, but resistance to taking the first step to procure this help often holds some people back. Are you resisting looking for help?

3. Save time by using marketing tools that allow you to reach many people all at once. Using social media and/or an email marketing program (like Constant Contact) can free up your time to do more of what you love.

NETWORKING

This is relevant for both in-person and online networking.

If we are here to help others, networking is key to reaching them. Not only does it increase awareness, education, and access to the products, services, and solutions you offer, but it helps you connect to the clients, customers, and patients who want your products, services, and help.

There are different places to network, depending on your primary purpose for networking. Choose with awareness, and you will get more from it.

These ideas will help you choose where to network, both in person and online. Where will you find the connections that can help you in each of the following five areas? They may be different groups. In some cases, there is likely to be overlap.

1. To get more clients, customers and patients.
2. To get referrals to more clients, customers, and patients. It's not just whether I am going to hire you. It's also who I know who may want to buy your products and/or services.
3. To attract more clients, customers, and patients through increased visibility. "Who did you see at last night's HCC meeting?" Also, groups that do social media posting and tagging after the meeting will be a boost for your online presence.
4. To get ideas for growing your business. There are so many elements of building a business (marketing and sales, time management, money management, customer service). Where do you go to come up with ideas and insights for making it easier?

I remember when an HCC member, a professional organizer and decluttering expert in a Texas chapter, was sitting next to an organic gardener and real estate agent. The realtor suggested she start visiting local real estate networking groups so she could meet more of the people who could introduce her to *their* clients, who always moved in and out of homes and offices. This is the rich vein of potential clients that would help her fill her time with paying clients who would value and appreciate her services. When one relationship allows you to connect easily with hundreds (or thousands), that's rich.

Keep in mind that it does *not* help you to add people to your email list without their permission. Some people prefer to follow you and get updates via social media. Others may not want what you are offering. No one wants to be nagged.

5. To find what you are looking for. What would happen if you went to a meeting looking for someone who was selling something that you wanted to buy? Would you start attracting people who are looking to buy what you sell? I have lost count of the number of times I've found a product or service provider, thanks to the HCC, and yes, I do pay for many of the products and services I want, even as I accept the gifts that are given.

Networking tips (especially for introverts): In a room full of people, I would rather have someone come to me than go to them. What about you?

1. Ask questions such as the following: How did you get started doing this? Why did you start this particular business? What do you like best about what you do? Tell me about your favorite client, customer, or patient.
2. Listen openly, not waiting to jump in with who you are, what you do, or giving your five-minute pitch.
3. Dress to blend in or to stand out. If you want people to approach you, you may want to stand out, rather than blending in. The easiest way is to wear a name badge.
4. Listen to self-introductions from the people you want to connect with, and then approach them at the end of the meeting.
5. Get business cards from those who have them.
6. Bring your business cards to give out to others.

7. A good group creates opportunities for easy interaction. We recommend a Q and A format for our chapters so that conversations are created more easily. Sharing our experiences leads to more insights, ideas, and inspiration for everyone.

Once you get back to your office:

1. Look people up on your favorite social media and connect there. I use Facebook and LinkedIn the most, although the HCC also has profiles on Twitter, Instagram, Pinterest, and YouTube.
2. If you got permission from new contacts, you can add them to your email list.
3. You also can send a one-time-only email with links to your website and social media, and see if they reply.

There are many ways to get value from networking, both online and in person. Creating rich relationships that go beyond the basics will help you expand in every element.

APPRECIATION AND ABUNDANCE

Be sure to appreciate and celebrate your transformation, starting with where you are today.

I invite you to join me in doing abundance.

THE A-BUN-DANCE

Love and Money do a little dance
Mix it up with a bit o' romance
That's what I call a-bun-dance
That's how I do a-bun-dance

WHERE YOU CAN FIND ME

https://CamilleLeon.com

https://HolisticChamberOfCommerce.com

https://Facebook.com/HolisticChamberOfCommerce

https://linkedin.com/in/camilleleon/

https://YouTube.com/HolisticCC

https://Instagram.com/HolisticChamber

https://pinterest.com/holisticchamberofcommerce1

Printed in the United States
By Bookmasters